My Parents Open Carry

An Open Carry Adventure!

Written by

Brian Jeffs
Nathan Nephew

Illustrated by

Lorna Bergman

Published by White Feather Press. (www.whitefeatherpress.com)

ISBN 978-1-6180810-1-8

Printed in the United States of America

White Feather Press

Reaffirming Faith in God, Family, and Country!

2nd Amendment

"A well regulated Militia, being necessary to the security of a free State, the right of the people to keep and bear Arms, shall not be infringed."

PREFACE

This book was written in the hope of providing a basic overview of the right to keep and bear arms as well as the growing practice of the open carry of a handgun. Our fear is that our children are being raised with a biased view of our constitution and especially in regards to the 2nd Amendment. Before writing this, we looked for pro-gun children's books and couldn't find any. Our goal is to provide a wholesome children's book that reflects the views of the majority of the American people, i.e., that self-defense is a basic natural right and that firearms provide the most efficient means for that defense. We truly hope you will enjoy this book and read and discuss it with your children over and over again.

Brian G. Jeffs & Nathan R. Nephew

Author's note to home school teachers: This book is an excellent text to use as a starting point on the discussion of the 2nd Amendment.

To

My wonderful daughter Brenna Lynn, I will love you forever.

Brian G. Jeffs

To

My parents for raising me with the values I hold today and to Christina and
KayleeAnna for sticking with me through all of the projects I involve myself in.

Nathan R. Nephew

Acknowledgments

I would like to thank Skip Coryell and White Feather Press for their belief in this work and for taking a chance and publishing this book. I hope we have a long relationship. I also want to thank Janet, my wife and Brenna, my daughter for their brutally honest reviews. I want to thank my mother, Julie and my late father, Francis, I'm grateful for all the things you both have done for me. Also my co-author Nate, thanks buddy, and get working on the next one. I would like to thank Oleg Volk for his reviews and comments. Lastly I want to thank you, the reader, for taking a stand in protecting not only the 2nd Amendment but all our rights. With people like you we will continue to live free and secure. Remember, the charge of every citizen of a free state is to be ever vigilant of our government's role as servant and never let it become our master.

Brian G. Jeffs 10/5/10

The Strong family consists of Richard Strong, his wife Bea and their 13 year old daughter, Brenna. The Strong family live in a modest home in a medium-sized town in the Midwest.

One morning, Brenna was sleeping and dreaming dreams only a 13 year old girl would dream, when she heard he mom say…"Brenna…honey…. wake up".

Brenna wasn't sure she heard her mom, so she rolled over and placed a pillow over her head. Brenna's mom said…"Brenna, come on Sweetheart, we have lots to do today. We have errands to run, people to see, and places to go!"

Brenna heard her mom this time and realized it was Saturday, and they did have a lot of plans today. Brenna got up and brushed her teeth and got dressed for the day. Since it was a warm day, she wore a green t-shirt, a pair of khaki shorts, and her favorite running shoes. When she went into the kitchen, her mom and dad were at the table eating breakfast. Brenna sat down and ate her cereal and toast and drank her apple juice as her parents discussed the day ahead.

The family was planning on going shopping and then to the bookstore, where they could look for books and CD's. Her dad also said that they were going somewhere special and it was a surprise. Brenna's parents were rewarding her for getting straight A's in school this year. Brenna asked her dad what the surprise was, but he wouldn't tell her. He said it was a secret.

When they were finished with breakfast, they cleared the plates and got ready to leave for the day. Brenna knew that her mom and dad had a ritual they always followed before they left the house. They retrieved their handguns from the locked gun safe and checked them to make sure they were loaded. They placed the handguns in their holsters that were in plain sight on their hips.

Brenna's parents were dressed casually. Her dad wore a white polo shirt with tan pants, a black belt and comfortable shoes. Her mom wore white cargo shorts and a nice shirt and her well worn brown loafers.

The family left the house, locked the door, and went to the car. As they walked to the car, Brenna could plainly see their handguns secured in their holsters on her parent's hips. She was reminded of what her mom and dad always told her. Dad would say, "Brenna, there is evil in this world, and we want to protect you the best we can." Mom would add, "We are responsible for our own safety, and as an adult, someday you will be responsible for your safety as well as your family." They both always added that the police do the best they can to protect us, but they can't be everywhere all the time. They both liked to say, "When seconds count, the police are minutes away."

Brenna thought they were right: a person that doesn't take on the responsibility for their own safety was not being true to nature's law. Everyone has the right, and the responsibility, to protect themselves and their loved ones from harm. Brenna thought it was strange that so many people don't understand this very simple truth.

Brenna's mom and dad both have concealed carry licenses so by state law they can carry a handgun loaded in a vehicle. As the family was about to climb into the car their next door neighbor, Mr. Wright waved good morning and said, "I see you both are packin' as usual. Good for you." He continued, "You just never know when you might need to protect yourself and loved ones. People wear seatbelts and have fire extinguishers. They hope to never need them, but it's best to be prepared I always say."

After Mr. Strong and Mr. Wright talked a bit, Mr. Wright said have a nice day and waved once again to the family as they buckled-up and drove away.

The first stop was J.G. Carol Hardware. Brenna's dad needed to buy nails for a bird house he was building. After parking the car, Brenna and her parents walked down the sidewalk to the store.

As they neared the store, a mother and her 6-year old child walked toward them. Brenna noticed that the woman was fearfully clutching her child. The woman commented, "What are you people doing? Guns in public are wrong. What about the children and my right to feel safe?" Brenna's dad and mom had heard these kinds of statements before. They try to inform these people with facts, not myths, about guns and gun safety. If the people listened, they tried to plant a seed of reason, but if they don't listen, well, there's not much else they can do.

Brenna's dad asked the women, "Why do you feel that guns in public are wrong?" The woman explained that guns are dangerous. They kill people, and only the military and police should have them. Brenna's dad stated that yes, guns can be dangerous and should be handled with care, but so should cars, chain saws, and many other tools that people use every day to make their lives better.

He went on to say that guns save far more lives than they take. In fact, he stated that merely displaying a gun can deter a crime from happening – which is why he carries his gun in the open. The woman hadn't thought about that. As she pondered these facts, and just before saying goodbye, Brenna's dad shared his favorite saying: "When seconds count, the police are minutes away."

After buying nails at the hardware store, they went to the grocery store. As the family was strolling down the fresh produce aisle, and Brenna's mom was explaining the health benefits of fresh spinach (as Brenna made yucky faces), an elderly man wearing an army veteran baseball cap approached them and thanked them for exercising their 2nd Amendment right.

The old man explained that he had fought in WWII to protect all of our rights, and he wished more people understood what freedom was. He looked at Brenna and went on to say that the 2nd Amendment, the one that states "A well regulated Militia being necessary for a free state, the right of the people to keep and bear arms shall not be infringed," wasn't about hunting or target shooting or even self defense.

He said the 2nd Amendment was spelled out to protect the people from a tyrannical government. The old veteran said that when the United States was forming a new government, the Founding Fathers knew that the surest way to keep the new republic from becoming too powerful was to allow the citizens the right to keep and bear arms. This assured that the new government wouldn't become too bossy, because the people had the means to fight against it. The veteran said, "A right unexercised is a right lost." He added that Brenna's mom was right and canned spinach was indeed good for you. Brenna's mom and dad agreed with a smile.

Now Brenna had heard all this before, but she still was a little confused about the "militia" part. She knew there was a National Guard. Wasn't that the "militia"? So she asked the nice man. The veteran said, "That's a good question. It confuses a lot of people, there are two classes of militia; organized and unorganized. The original militia was unorganized which included every man (and today every woman) aged 17 to 45 that were fit enough for active service to defend their town, their state, and their country from attack. In other words the "militia" is everyday citizens like your mom and dad." The organized militia is the National guard and Naval Militias.

Brenna thought about this for a moment, and then it clicked! In fact, it made perfect sense: the "militia" and the "people" are the same thing. The 2nd Amendment was about the right of the "people" to keep and bear arms. Brenna's dad added that for many years some Americans couldn't exercise their 2nd Amendment rights. It was only in 2009 that the US Supreme Court ruled that the right to keep and bear arms was an <u>individual</u> right, and in 2010 the High Court ruled that the 2nd Amendment was incorporated to the states. That means that the states have to abide by the Second Amendment just like many other rights.

The Strong family went across the square to the Sheridan Bookstore. This was Brenna's favorite store in town. Brenna made a beeline right to the music section. Brenna's parents went in different directions; both of them loved to read, and so they looked for a book to buy.

After they browsed the shelves, Brenna's parents sat down in the bookstore's café and talked. Several shoppers wandered the aisles, looking at the wide selection of books and CDs. After a few minutes, a man approached Brenna's parents and asked if he could talk to them about their handguns. Brenna's dad said, "Sure. What would you like to know?" "Well," the man said, "I have a concealed pistol permit, and I always carry my handgun concealed and out of sight. I keep a shirt or jacket over my handgun at all times." "That's good," said Brenna's dad. Brenna's parents didn't care if people chose to open carry or conceal carry as long as they carried and were responsible. Her parents would sometimes conceal carry as well. It's nice to have the option to do either.

The man stated that he didn't open carry because he felt he would be the first person shot if something bad like a bank robbery went down. Brenna's dad grinned a bit; he had heard this myth several times when it came to open carry versus concealed carry.

Brenna's dad told the man that he had never heard of a person openly carrying a handgun being a target or shot during a robbery. This was an image portrayed in TV and movies. In fact, there is more evidence to suggest that people who open carry a handgun deter crimes from happening in the first place. There are several cases of robbers who staked out a store to rob only to go somewhere else because they saw someone with a gun in the store.

"In fact, I had this exact thing happen to me. One morning last summer, my friend and I were sitting in Woodruff's Waffle World on Main St. eating breakfast. As usual, I was open carrying my handgun. Beaing aware of my surroundings, I noticed a man come into the restaurant and look all around like he was looking for somebody. This seemed a bit suspicious to me so I kept my eye on him and what was going on around us. The man looked at me, glanced down and quickly went back outside. We left Waffle World, almost forgetting about the suspicious man. Later that night on the news I heard that the local police had stopped two men in a suspicious vehicle behind that restaurant and the men admitted to planning a robbery that very morning. The men commented that they decided not to rob Woodruff's because they saw a customer armed with a gun on his hip. I believe the customer they saw was me.

Brenna's dad continued, "Criminals like a "soft target" - a target that won't put up a fight. Criminals don't want to face a person who is armed or might be armed. The US Department of Justice interviewed convicted robbers on this subject, and the majority agreed. They want easy targets for crime. So, it may be to your advantage to open carry. It's like a "beware of dog" sign. It says don't mess with me, I'll fight back."

"Well," the man said, "maybe you're right about that, but if you open carry a handgun someone could come up behind you and steal it away from you." "Yes, I suppose that could happen," said Brenna's mom, "But we have never heard of this happening to a citizen. It has happened to police officers because they have to sometimes fight and struggle with criminals that are desperate to get away. And it could happen to a citizen as well, that's why we have good retention holsters."

Brenna's mom continued, "Our holsters are designed to only allow the person that is carrying the handgun to draw it. This allows you time to react to an attempted gun snatch. We also stay aware of our surroundings." Brenna's dad added, "Everyone should be aware of their surroundings and other people around them. Crime and evil can happen anywhere at anytime, history shows that."

To increase Brenna's awareness, her dad often tries to sneak up on her to catch her off guard; it's a game they play. If she catches him he has to do the dishes that night. If she doesn't, then she has to do the dishes.

"What about brandishing?" The man asked. He continued and said "I have heard that having a gun in a holster is brandishing." Brenna's dad said "We hear that a lot, but it's not true. Brandishing is waving or pointing your gun in a threatening manner, or emphasizing you're armed in an attempt to intimidate someone. Just wearing a gun in a holster is not brandishing."

The man said he had a lot to think about and would give open carry more thought. Brenna's mom said that many people start out thinking open carry is not for them and that's okay, but many decide to give it a try after they research it and think about it more. The man thanked them for the information and said he would definitely do both. The man and Brenna's parents shook hands, and the man walked back to his family.

As Brenna continued to shop, some teenagers who were curious about her parents' handguns approached them and asked if the guns were real. "Yes," said Brenna's mom, "they're real." "Cool!" said the boy. "Yeah pretty cool," said the girl. "My dad has hunting rifles," said the young girl "He hunts deer." Brenna's parents both nodded and said they too, hunt deer up north.

The boy asked them why they carry their handguns out in the open. "That's a good question," said Mr. Strong. "There are many reasons. Open carry can deter a crime, it's a faster draw, and it's more comfortable in the summer when we wear light clothing. It also brings gun ownership out of the closet and into the mainstream and shows the public that good people keep and bear arms. It lets people know that their neighbors, pastors, doctors, lawyers, and friends bear arms. It lets people realize that guns don't have to always be related to crime. It shows that guns are not evil. Some people do evil things – that's the problem."

The teens talked a little more about guns and hunting, and then they left to do more shopping. Brenna came back and said she was ready to learn what the surprise was.

Brenna's parents laughed and said, "All right, I think we can do that." So they went to their car and got in. They buckled up and off they drove. After 20 minutes or so, they were in the country. Brenna had been down this road before, and she thought she knew where they were going. A few minutes more and Brenna's dad made a turn down a two-track road. Now Brenna knew for sure that they were going to the shooting range. She and her family often went to the range so that her parents could keep up their shooting skills and teach Brenna gun safety. "What is special about this?" Brenna thought, "This isn't special." She was beginning to feel disappointed, but she didn't say anything.

At the range, Brenna and her dad reviewed the basic rules of safe gun handling.

ALWAYS keep the gun pointed in a safe direction.
ALWAYS keep your finger off the trigger until ready to shoot.
ALWAYS keep the gun unloaded until ready to use.

After following all of the firearm safety rules, the Strong family set up at one of the benches. Brenna's dad laid out both his and Brenna's mom's handguns on the bench, making sure they were both safely pointed downrange.

Mr. Strong was reaching into his brown leather shooting bag when Mr. Freeman, the range officer, stopped by and said hello. Mr. Strong and Mr. Freeman chatted a bit, and soon the topic turned to guns and self defense. Brenna's dad and Mr. Freeman were always discussing the topic of open carry versus concealed carry. Mr. Freeman taught concealed pistol classes and self-defense courses for men and woman. Mr. Freeman didn't open carry his handgun, preferring to conceal it. But he did mention that he was seeing more and more responsible adults open carrying in town and that it seemed to be catching on.

Mr. Strong often discussed the advantages of open carry as a crime deterrent. He liked to give this example. If a person is concealing his handgun and walking across a dark parking lot a mugger assumes he is helpless, he approaches the concealed carrier and says "Give me your wallet and you wont get hurt". The victim has some choices to make, but the sensible one is to hand over your wallet and stay alert. The mugger takes the wallet and runs off. The victim could pull his handgun and shoot at the mugger as he runs away, but generally this would not be a justifiable use of a firearm, so he can only call 911 and report the crime.

Then Mr. Strong said that if the victim wore his gun in the open chances are good that the mugger would have waited until he found a "softer target" to rob. Criminals don't like armed victims.
By open carrying a handgun, the person avoids becoming a victim all together. Mr. Freeman nodded his head slowly, "Perhaps you're right."
The two men chatted a bit more then shook hands and said goodbye.

Brenna was getting impatient. "What was the surprise?" she wondered. She asked her mom what was so special about the shooting range; they come here all the time. Brenna's mom and dad exchanged glances and grinned. "All right, Brenna." "Show her," Brenna's mom said to her dad. So Brenna's dad reached into his shooting bag, took out a gun case, set it on the bench, and opened it. Inside was a brand new handgun that Brenna had never seen before. She was starting to get excited. Was this a new handgun for her mom or her dad? She had to ask, "Mom whose handgun is that? It looks great!" Brenna's mom and dad both answered at the same time, "It's yours!, you deserve it for getting such great grades in school". Brenna couldn't believe it. Brenna thought...my own handgun!

"Well, it will be yours when you turn 18," said Brenna's dad. "In our state, you have to be at least 18 years old to own a pistol, but you can shoot it with your mom and me today. In fact, we got it for you so you could practice with us when we go to the range." "What do you think?" asked Brenna's mom. "Do you like it?" "Like it?" Brenna said, "I love it!" "Dad can I shoot it today?" "Sure," said her dad, "I was hoping you would ask."

For over an hour, Brenna's dad taught her the workings of her new pistol, and they practiced shooting targets. On the way home, the Strongs discussed the day. They talked about how important the right to keep and bear arms is and how it should always be protected. They also discussed how people have a responsibility to protect themselves and their loved ones from harm, and the best tool for personal defense is a handgun, whether carried openly or concealed as allowed by law.

All in all, Brenna had a great day with her mom and dad. She again realized how much they loved her and how lucky she was to have parents that open carry.

The Authors

BRIAN G. JEFFS, is a senior geologist with the state of Michigan. Brian is the Co-founder of Michigan Open Carry, Inc., a non-profit organization that promotes the open carry of a handgun and works to protect all firearm rights. Brian is also on the Board of Directors for the Second Amendment March, a non-profit pro-gun organization that organized the first pro-2nd Amendment rally in Washington D.C. in 2010. He is co-host of the Saturday Afternoon Shootout, an internet talk show on the 2nd Amendment. His love and respect for firearms and the 2nd amendment began at an early age and were nurtured by his father. Brian is married, has a daughter, as well as a dog and a cat. He enjoys hunting, fishing and living free.

NATHAN R. NEPHEW is a software developer and co-founder of Michigan Open Carry, Inc., a non-profit organization that promotes the open carry of a handgun and works to protect all firearm rights. His knowledge and love of firearms came from his parents. His strong passion for the 2nd Amendment began after realizing that American's rights are slowly being stripped away. Nathan graduated from Kettering University with a Bachelors in Computer Engineering. He lives in DeWitt, MI and enjoys hunting, fishing, and playing the drums in several bands. My Parents Open Carry is his first book.

The Artist

Lorna Bergman is a Michigan artist and has worked in various mediums. She is a hunter and enjoys shooting and deer hunting.

GLOSSARY OF TERMS:

Brandishing: **1.** To wave or flourish (a weapon, for example) menacingly. **2.** To display ostentatiously. A legal term for waving around a weapon in a threatening manner.

Concealed carry: A manner of carrying a weapon on ones body in a way that is out of sight. For example, to carry a handgun inside the waistband covered by a shirt or jacket. Could also include carrying a handgun in a purse or backpack.

Easy target: Someone that would be easy to rob. For example an elderly person, a woman, a person that is preoccupied or one that appears to be unarmed and wouldn't cause much trouble during the crime.

Incorporated: The incorporation of the Bill of Rights is the process by which American courts have applied portions of the U.S. Bill of Rights to the states. Prior to the 1890s, the Bill of Rights was held only to apply to the federal government. Under the incorporation doctrine, most provisions of the Bill of Rights now also apply to the state and local governments, by virtue of the due process clause of the Fourteenth Amendment of the Constitution.

Militia: From the US CODE-TITLE 10 > Subtitle A > PART I > CHAPTER 13 > § 311 § 311. Militia: composition and classes

(a) The militia of the United States consists of all able-bodied males at least 17 years of age and, except as provided in section 313 of title 32, under 45 years of age who are, or who have made a declaration of intention to become, citizens of the United States and of female citizens of the United States who are members of the National Guard.

(b) The official classes of the militia are—

(1) the organized militia, which consists of the National Guard and the Naval Militia; and

(2) the unorganized militia, which consists of the members of the militia who are not members of the National Guard or the Naval Militia.

Mugger: A slain term for a criminal that robs people. A mugger may use force or intimidation to rob someone.

Nature's law: Idea of perfect law based on the concept that all men are created equal and should be treated with fairness. Natural law is based on the idea that the universe and all physical laws can be applied to human behavior and which can be deduced through reasoning and the sense of what is right or wrong.

Open carry: To carry a handgun uncovered and in the open such as in a holster and worn on the hip.

Packin': Slang for carrying a gun. Can be used in reference to either concealed or open carry. 'That man is packin' a gun."

Retention holster: A holster designed to keep the handgun in it until it is drawn by the person carrying it. Generally these holsters use a mechanism that has to be activated in order to draw the gun. Some retention holsters use a strap that has to be unsnapped to draw the handgun.

Situational awareness: To be aware of your surrounding. This is desired to prevent a criminal the opportunity to catch you unaware. People that are more aware of what is going on around them are less likely to be a victim of crime.

Tyrannical: a person or government that acts like a tyrant. Tyrant: **1.** An absolute ruler who governs without restrictions. **2.** A ruler who exercises power in a harsh, cruel manner. **3.** An oppressive, harsh, arbitrary person.

CPSIA information can be obtained at www.ICGtesting.com
Printed in the USA
LVOW10s2018110814

398593LV00028B/1204/P